A Journal of Photography & Poetry

FOCUS

SUMMER 2019

FOUNDER & MANAGING EDITOR
Jennifer Drucker

POETRY EDITOR
Manny Blacksher

MAILING ADDRESS
PO BOX 420, SMITHTOWN, NY 11787

WEBSITE
WWW.LIGHT-JOURNAL.COM

IN THIS ISSUE | FOCUS

A Note From the Editor

"When words become unclear, I shall focus with photographs. When images become inadequate, I shall be content with silence."
-Ansel Adams

Regardless of what we, as individuals are passionate about, we need to gift ourselves the time to focus on it. Make the time to do it. Easier said than done, I know. It has been a while since I picked up my camera and I need to. I need to focus on it once again. When I ignore it, the thoughts slowly raise their volume, screaming until they are deafening.

I think most artists feel this way. Life can get so overwhelming for all of us, but it is through our art that we find our happiness, our silence, our peace.

Thank you for your continued support of *Light*.

Warm regards,

Jennifer Drucker
Founder & Managing Editor

JENNIFER WALKER | *From Here & There*

T.L. MURPHY | *She Holds On*

She holds what's left
when moments wing
a name, a number
a time, a place
for keeping ordinary things.

She wants to know
who let the damn
cat out
now that chickens
have come home to the goose.

There's a breeze
in the back of the room
a certain shadow
at dirty bottom
where corners converge

and birds mark
empty space in the overcast sky
flying from flat horizons
just below
sightless eyes.

She holds on to mind's mirage
each bird a boat, a personal
flotation device, a rapidly
vanishing point
she wanted to make.

STEPHEN EIDSEN | *Snagged*

PATRICIA JOYNES | *Bass Lake Reflection*

KATHIE GIORGIO | *Comma*

Through history and lives,
and loves,
in letters, telegrams, postcards,
emails, tweets and texts,
a proper comma keeps thousands
from speaking the truth.
From letting hearts spell
their full request:
Love, Me (we signed)
Love Me (we said)

CHRIS SEID | *Ghost Roses*

MEGAN MERCHANT | *Vase for the Dead*

I wake exhausted,
unable to find
my mother in dreams.

I pick from a jar of river
rocks, suck one,
sharpen my teeth.

Even cold, my coffee
tastes like rust.
At noon, I lean my head

against a man's chest,
tell him about
javelina that scavenge

our trash in the night.
How they scrub
for seeds and how, last

summer, I planted
a dozen tulips
that were beheaded

by morning. He kisses
me hard, says, *that
should be placed somewhere*

in the body. He means
of a poem. I bite
my lip until it bleeds.

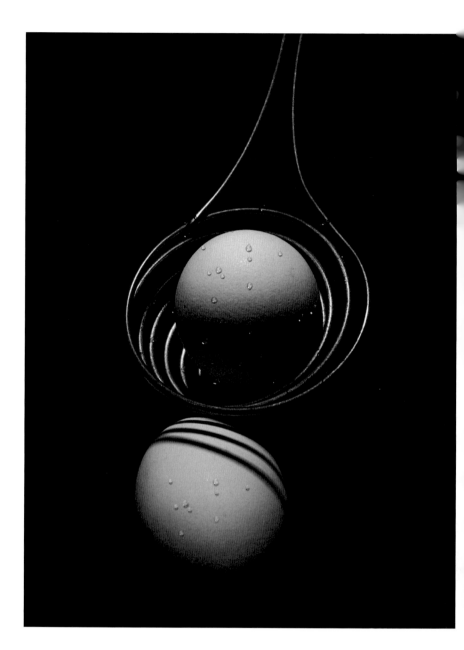

KARI GUNTER-SEYMOUR | *Still Life With Water*

KARI GUNTER-SEYMOUR | *Silent Killer*

CHARLOTTE HOBBS | *Untitled from the series The Cold and Solitude of Friends of Mine*

WONJUNE KIM | *HiGi*

FRANCES BOYLE | *Attentive*

Swirls of tension
dissolve into pure green light
as filtered by oak and maple leaves
as filtered by stream water running
green over mossy logs. The sound
of the ravens a green not crystalline
but faceted, broken into angles as if
the cry is breaking their bird throats,
croak pulled as on a string, a singing
guttural in ancient huffs, antiphonal
call and response. Green dragonfly ranks
weaving air over grass into summer twilight.
The concussion of a loon's wings as it lifts and rides
the water beating beating air. A rabbit's ears, its only
moving part, like purposeful antennae-dishes swivel,
scan. The heron overhead, wings wide, feet dangling,
the intensity of the dog's watching the bird as it lands,
stands stockstill until striking for minnow or tadpole.

MANTZ YORKE | *Photoshoot, Dungeness*

A couple in a dilapidated hut:
he is taking photographs while she
poses on the surviving shelf.
I imagine the aesthetic –

slats blown from walls and roof
letting stripes of sunlight undulate
across her smooth brown skin:
as I come near she cups a hand
over a naked breast.

I see my photograph –

empty hut with rusty rails leading
across shingle to a decaying boat,
but hold off, taking instead rivets
dotting the boat's ash-grey strakes.
They go: I take a last opportunity

to shoot this dereliction.
Winter will blow down the hut:
its timbers will soon be rotting,
junk food for the stones.

GREG ZECK | *Cloudless Sulphur*
(For Dorothy Mangold)

The light was perfect this afternoon,
you said, on Clabber Creek when
you went out with your Nikon
and the uxorious lemon-yellow
lepidopteron, the Cloudless Sulphur
(Phoebis sennae), presented himself,
nectaring on our noxious native thistle,
feeding at his leisure and only then
darting home to his paler mate.
Dorothy, photographer of light,
master of the evanescent moment
when papery creatures might be
f-stopped down in flight or feeding
when they light on partridge peas,
Bahama cassia, wild senna, petunias,
honeysuckles, our native thistle,
employing their extra long proboscis
as you employ your extra long lens,
your extra patient habit of simply looking,
focusing, abiding quietly in one place
before you too take flight.

DAN O'CONNELL | *Divisadero Thoughts*

watch from window
filthy shoeless man

on meth bender
whip around every

parking meter
shouting "Stop following me!"

to empty sidewalk
so go on Facebook
and unfollow
my old friend Bob

CLAYTON JOE YOUNG | *Permanent Records*

JAN BALL | *Dad's Necklace*

After Mom and Dad's divorce,
at first, I didn't want to invite
my friends to Dad's on the days
I'm with him because he sometimes
dresses like a girl: He wears a skirt
with big flowers on it, and a blouse
with ruffles and puffy sleeves
like Mom wears.

When my friends come over,
Dad sometimes puts on a necklace
with his Chicago Bulls t-shirt, too.

But now I don't care because he's
still my Dad and, anyway,
my fifth grade friends joke with him,
"Hey, Mr. Abbott, can I wear
your necklace while I'm here?"
(It seems like they really want to)

Then, he throws a football with us
in the yard like he always did.
I know Mom thinks there's something
wrong about it but it's ok with me.

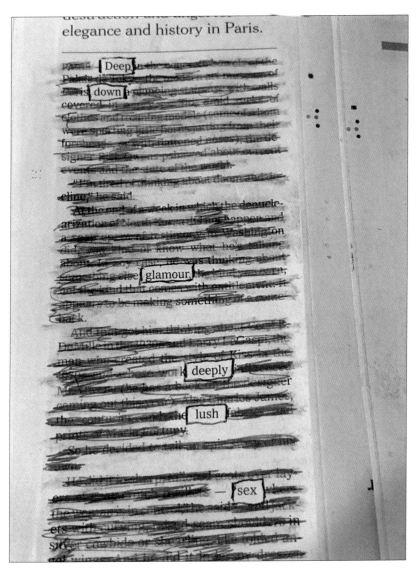

elegance and history in Paris.

Deep down glamour deeply lush — sex

MARY JOHANSEN | *Found Poem No. 1*

EMMA FILTNESS | *Rolleiflex Women*
after Diane Arbus: in the beginning *at Hayward Gallery*

I am the headless woman
and a girl in her circus costume backstage

I am the old woman in a hospital bed
and a disinterred saint in her glass and gold casket

I am the woman in white fur with a cigarette
and a seated female impersonator with arms crossed on her bare chest

I am the blurry woman gazing up smiling
and a stripper with bare breasts sitting in her dressing room

I am the woman with a crescent rhinestone brooch
and a lady who appears to be a gentleman

I am the screaming woman with blood on her hands
and every blonde on screen about to be kissed

CHEN XIANGYUN | *Untitled*

UZOMAH UGWU | *A Child's Harmony (for Vincent)*

He held his guitar like a woman on the verge

Of a still birth and in such hardship, her own welfare stared back at him

Chord for chord it was like he was birthing the child for new air

His harmonies outlasted the night filled with trauma it was

The kind of brightness that brought light to lampposts

In a hurry, he gathered his guitar close like he knew note for note his job

Had begun to overshadow what it was meant for

With all eyes on him and the storms of people begging for an encore

He reached out his hand and bowed to an audience that

For a few hours felt what was in his heart and as he left the stage

His song fell apart into a mother's arms where there was a child all

From the extension of his arms that explained why he did perform

MD SABBIR | Untitled

LOUIS STAEBLE | *Soft Turn*

DIANA COLE | *Mullein*

Ripped from its rosette, the leaf
lies in my hand, light as a butterfly.
Its surface that seems crushed
velvet, is in fact resilient —spikes
that bend and spring back.
To touch the nap is to suspect how
my grandmother recovered,
hid her grievance in decorum.

This weed that grows in disturbed soil
exacts full sun. Its wayfaring
hardiness dodges shade. Which is
to suspect why she never spoke
of his breakdowns, but held herself upright
just as the Mullein stalk reaches above snow
so that blossoms fused at its base
will burst into their fervent yellow lives.

MEMYE CURTIS TUCKER | *We Walked with You Across the Campus*
(for Denise Levertov)

When we passed the black tulips,
you left us for those petals,
velvet, shimmering purple,
looked long into their hearts'
charcoal. You returned to us,
burning.

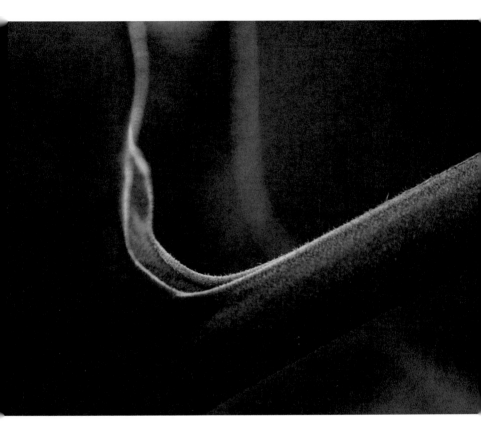

MARY GERAKARIS | *Botanical Dance*

FRANK ROSSINI | *My Mother 1923 (Imogen Cunningham)*

she stands in front of the barnwood wall
illumined with unfocused light drifting
like steam from the pail brimmed
with morning's milk she holds
in the crook of her right arm her right
hand fingers spread presses
the bucket's weight against her clean
ironed apron she wears
over a collared striped long-
sleeved dress her left hand deep
in the apron's pocket

the right side of her face & hair
is washed with early light
the center & left side gently shadowed
her mouth turned down
at the corners her eyes
serious with a hint
of impatience behind
her rimless glasses say
there is always
work to do

her daughter says
"Mother was very difficult
to photograph"

PAULINE FLYNN | *On a Sudden Impulse*

Joan glances around before opening
the umbrella inside the restaurant.

She knows she shouldn't offer herself up
to superstitious glares, even attack,

but she feels pissed off about everything;
the inattentive service of the waiter,

the noise from the coffee machine
pelleting her brain, the surge

of electric current in her body, burning.
It's the slow slide into the invisible

vexes her the most and she isn't having it.
She stands up, pushes the chair away,

holds the umbrella upright like a sword,
triggers the spring. She feels the snap

of ribs against the umbrella's canopy,
the rush of air, and all eyes on her.

AFIEYA KIPP | *Hero*

this is my favorite photograph—before our relationships became something of the earth in a place where things don't grow, and the humming of a Benz motor was the 'cross' in a useless exorcism of a paranoid black girl, and wet towels saved almost severed heads from rolling down carpeted steps, and the odor of old Big Mac containers put me to sleep, and I navigated the narrow hallways of our bunker—i mean 'home'—saving everyone from the Big Bad Tom Cat—it is me, pointing to the camera wearing a tiny pink pajama set, guzzling bedtime stories about order in utero.

TONY BRANDSTETTER | *Sing*

XE M. SÁNCHEZ | *Unfocused*

Poems
use magic glasses
to see the souls
of men and women.
This is your poem.
It is an infocused poem.
Don't worry.
It is said that time
is the best healer.

MARGARITA SERAFIMOVA | *Untitled (At the grand feast...)*

At the grand feast of the people and August, you are present –
absent-minded and concentrated.
I am in your heart,
and it hinders you from stepping light-mindedly.
You love. Summer is burning for another end.

PETER WHELAN | *Converging*

PHOTOGRAPHY
Featured Portfolio

NATHALIE DAOUST | *Transition*

NATHALIE DAOUST | *Transition*

Statement

Tent City consists of 35 images depicting Mongolian nomads who are forced to relocate from the steppe to the polluted outskirts of the capital Ulaanbaatar due to climate change drastically affecting their rural sustainability. Mongolian nomads are extremely environmentally conscious and generate little to no waste. Now many migrate to the Ger District, an area that is overcrowded, leading to severe lack of sewerage, water facilities and central heating. Thus, cheap coal is burnt to keep warm, which generates fatal pollution adding to rapidly increasing climate change that, as a result, threatens the nomads' livelihood on the steppe. My project photographically documents over two months the irreversible transformation of an ancient tradition and its shift to modernity, capturing the nomads' entire journey from rural to urban and how they adapt to the challenges and perks of modernization.

Biography

 A graduate of the Cégep du Vieux in Montreal, Canadian photographer Nathalie Daoust, first caught public attention in 1999 with her surreal series New York Hotel Story. This sequence of photographs investigates the Carlton Arms Hotel's 54 uniquely decorated rooms. The resultant images establish Daoust as a photographer capable of cutting beneath the surface to expose her subject's hidden desires. Her images are portals, allowing the viewer to get a glimpse of a world divorced from reality, one that flickers from childlike wonderment to perversion.

Daoust is led by her need to understand the human impulse to construct experiences that allow us to live, at least for a moment, in a fictive world. From female dominatrices at an S&M Love Hotel in Japan in Tokyo Hotel Story, to one man's decision to discard his own identity in favor of another in Impersonating Mao, her work inhabits the liminal space between fiction and truth. Her most conceptually complex project to date, Korean Dreams, explores the meaning of fantasy itself. While in North Korea she experienced the manipulation of reality on a national scale; her photographs capture the layers of forced illusion perpetuated by the North Korean government.

- Samantha Small

POETRY
Featured Collection

CHRISTOPHER SEID

CHRISTOPHER SEID | *Biography*

Christopher Seid is a freelance writer, experimental photographer and the author of two award-winning books of poetry, *Prayers to the Other Life* and *Age of Exploration*. Originally from the Midwest, he has lived in New York and New England for over 30 years—dividing his time now between Cambridge, Massachusetts and Portland, Maine.

Dissed

You can spend years looking
over that wound, in isolation,
licking your room. Only
your former classmates,
flipping through back and white
pages of yearbook windows,
care—unconscious or not
of the blacklit noon.
No one asks to be hurt
like that, on the receiving end
of a metaphorical bitchslap.
It's your test to touch the edge
with the toe of your boot
and miss the shifting sea—
cumulus clouds accumulating
like egrets of foam
on a wheezing tide. It's okay
to carry that burn as a crescendo,
birthmark that never deflates.
It's your right to trade, to toss
in a hole all the pain
of a star's stain—five-fingered
floodrush, nickprint on
the bleeding page.

Vespas

Evening dawns. Everything stalls.
A husk of landscape shucked
from cobble and copse, smoldering snow
thrashed in the daily wisp of willows.

What dies? What lies? What dries out?
Fires flying in the eyes of those men
who comb the cropped grass for grubs,
the distant highway's diminishing whine

and circumnavigational rhymes.
Everything slows—but everything sings.
Coals seethe long after their tender's retired,
smoke sags like a banner over an empty stage.

The hollow dark. The holler darker.
How long has the audience been asleep?

Everyone Has a Father Somewhere

Everyone has a father somewhere, but not everyone knows
his name. Even if the two of you shared a small house
on Cape Cod for 20 years, he may be no more present in your life
than a streak of milky water sponged on a picture window.

And to think all this time you were never properly
introduced, knowing each other instead by
the occasional yellow sticky note on the refrigerator
with steps on how to use the coffee pot,

or a number to call in case of emergency. Some afternoons,
returning from a walk on the beach, you might have felt a hand
brush your shoulder as you removed your shoes—
and later notice a sandy residue on your sweater, wondering:

Is he close? Had he just been here, searching the house
for you—his tumbler of pale whiskey and ice still shivering
on the coffee table? Perhaps he'd come to surprise you
but only found this salty light foaming in the flowing tide?

Or, could it be you're the one who's invisible?
And returning from your walk, the door sliding shut
without a nudge, you hear shuffling in the room above,
an errant coin drop with a "plunk" on the floor—a half-dollar,

like one your father pulled from his pocket of loose change
when he was 12 or 13. You never knew him
like this, but the evidence is everywhere:
sink full of dishes, empty coffee cup on the counter,

pearl tie clasp on the mantel where you always look first.
Everyone has a father somewhere, but not every father knows
his child—after she has grown up, married, and moved away
to raise her own little one, a daughter like you.

—for JF

Maine Midwinter

Stop-action waves of frozen snow.
Trees, like pilings of a pier, holding up
a platform of rickety stars.

What can we do now but wait
for thaw, every day an increment
warmer—gradual ratchet of photons,

clickless, a cutout sun raised on ropes
midway through the production of
a middle school play? Hard

to imagine summer—when everything
flows on the inside, ebbs on the out:
from flapping sheets on the clothesline

to the yawning leaf. What can prayer
accomplish at this point—
aren't we already dead and buried

at the bottom of this bitter cold?
Or are we only paused, poised
and waiting to slip out of our skin—our

dreamstate—not yet awake enough
to kick off the quilts and tumble outside
into high heat and bristling noon.

Made in the USA
Middletown, DE
05 April 2023

28280249R00035